Bathtime

Gill Tanner and Tim Wood

Photographs by Maggie Murray

Illustrations by Pat Tourret

A & C Black · London

Here are some of the people you will meet in this book.

The Hart family in 1990

The Cook family in 1960

Lee Hart is the same age as you.
His sister Kerry is eight years old.
What is Lee's mum called?

This is Lee's mum Linda when she
was just nine years old in 1960.
She is with her mum and dad,
her brother and her baby sister.

The Smith family in 1930

Richard Smith

Lucy Smith

May

Jack and June

The Barker family in 1900

Charles Barker

Alice Barker

Fred

Harry

Lucy

Amy and Adam

This is Lee's granny June
when she was just a baby in 1930.
Her brother Jack is looking after her.

This is Lee's great grandma Lucy
when she was six years old in 1900.
Can you see what her sister
and her brothers are called?

3

Can you spot the differences between these two photographs?

One shows bathtime in a modern house
and one shows bathtime
one hundred years ago.

This book is about bathtime and washing.
It will help you find out how bathtime
and washing have changed in the last
one hundred years.

There are twelve mystery objects in this book
and you can find out what they are.
They will tell you a lot about people in the past.

In 1900, this mystery object was used
by the Barker children at bathtime.
It's big enough to sit in.
Can you guess why it needed handles?

Turn the page to find out.

This is the Barkers' kitchen one hundred years ago.
Can you spot the mystery object? It's a **tin bath**.
In those days only very rich people had bathrooms.
The Barker children had to bath in the kitchen.

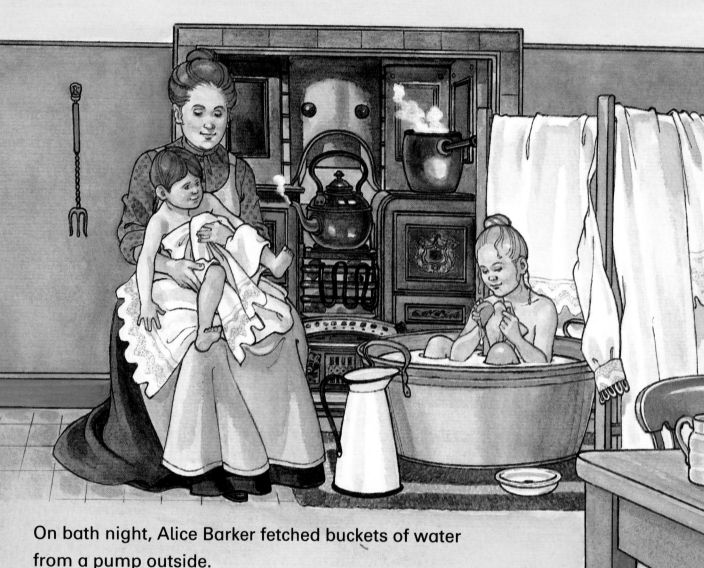

On bath night, Alice Barker fetched buckets of water
from a pump outside.
She heated the water in saucepans on the kitchen range.
Then she fetched the tin bath from outside the house
and filled it with hot water.
All the children used the same water.
When everyone had bathed, the dirty water
was tipped into a gutter outside.

This mystery object is made of metal.
It is about the same size as a watering can
but it has three handles.
Alice Barker carried it upstairs at night.
Can you guess what is inside?

Turn the page to find out.

Can you spot the mystery object?
It's a **hot-water can**.

Alice and Charles bathed
in a hip bath in their bedroom.
It was called a hip bath because when they sat in it
the water only came up to their hips.
Alice and Charles used the water can to carry
hot water upstairs from the kitchen to fill the bath.
They carried the dirty water downstairs in buckets.
Preparing for a bath was very hard work.

This mystery object is
about the same size as a pudding bowl.
It is made of china.
The top part has holes in it
and lifts off from the bottom part.

Turn the page to find out what it is.

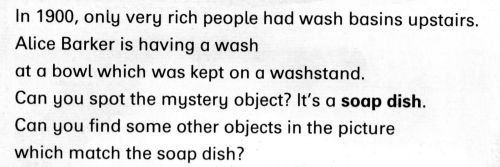

In 1900, only very rich people had wash basins upstairs.
Alice Barker is having a wash
at a bowl which was kept on a washstand.
Can you spot the mystery object? It's a **soap dish**.
Can you find some other objects in the picture
which match the soap dish?

The holes in the top of the soap dish let the water drain
through so the soap did not go soggy.
When she had finished washing, Alice took the dirty water
downstairs in a slop bucket.

Charles Barker used these
three things every morning.
The longest object is about
the same size as one of your belts.
Can you guess what the objects are?

Turn the page to find out.

The mystery objects are a **strop**, a **shaving mug** and a **cut-throat razor**.
Charles Barker used them when he shaved.

First he sharpened the blade of the razor on a leather strap called a strop.

Then he used a shaving brush and a piece of shaving soap to lather his face around his beard. Charles kept the brush, soap and hot water for shaving in his shaving mug.

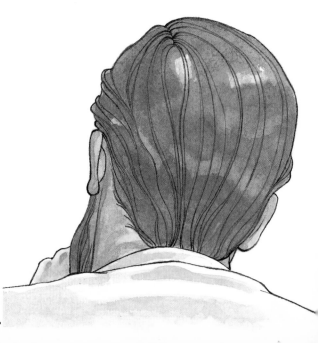

Charles shaved using a cut-throat razor. He shaved around the top of his beard and under his mouth.
The blade of the razor was very sharp.
Charles had to be careful not to cut his face.

In 1930, this mystery object made bathtime
a lot easier for the Smith family.
It is about as tall as you are.
It is made of metal.
What do you think it did?

Turn the page to find out.

This is bathtime at the Smiths' house in 1930.
How is it different from bathtime at the Barkers'?
Can you spot the mystery object?
It's called a **geyser**.

Jack waited in the bathroom whilst his dad ran the bath.
The geyser used gas to heat the water.
When Richard Smith turned on the tap,
flames lit inside the geyser and heated the water.
The hot water came out of the spout at the front.
The geyser made a roaring noise.
Jack thought it sounded like a dragon!

14

The Smiths used these when they bathed.
You can probably guess what the smaller object is.
The other object is about as long as your arm
from the elbow to your fingertips.

Turn the page to find out what they are.

Jack is having a bath.
Can you see the mystery objects?
They are a **loofah** and **carbolic soap**.

Jack used the loofah to scrub his back.
He made a soapy lather with carbolic soap.
A strong disinfectant in carbolic soap killed germs.
But it made the soap smell horrible.
Do you have a loofah in your bathroom?
Do you know what it is made of?

In 1960, the Cook family used this at bathtime.

It is a bit longer than one of your arms.

You may have something like it in your bathroom.

Do you know what it is made of?

Turn the page to find out what it is.

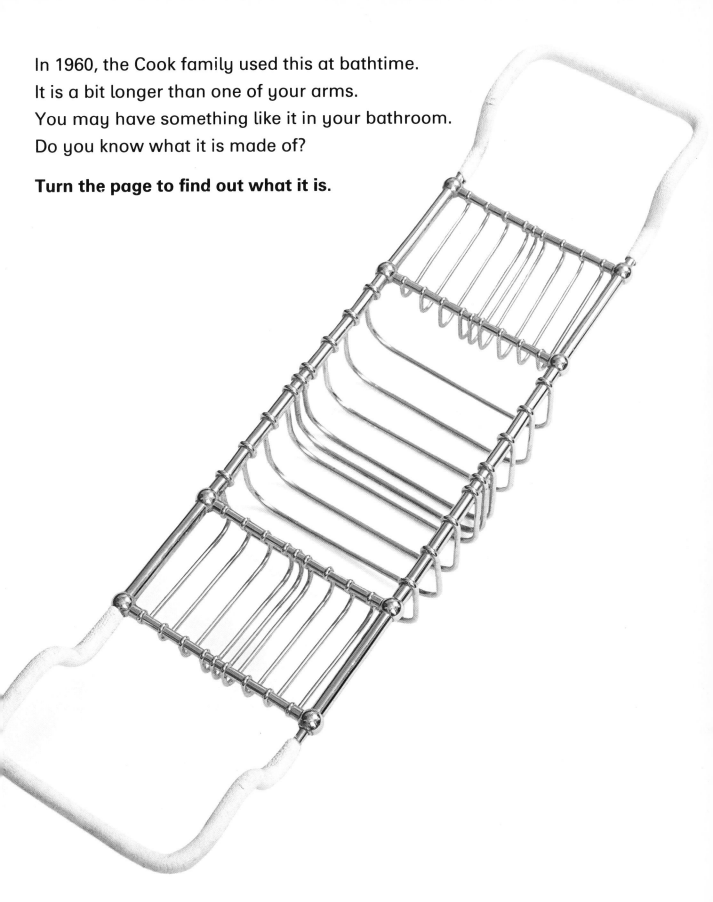

This is the Cooks' bathroom in 1960.
How is it different from the Smiths' bathroom?
Can you spot the mystery object?
It's a **bath rack**.

Linda has a friend staying the night.
They are having a bath.
Linda keeps her flannel, the soap and her rubber duck
on the bath rack where she can reach them easily.
This bath rack is made of metal.
Do you have a bath rack in your bathroom?
What do you keep on it?

This mystery object is made of metal.
Do you have something like it in your bathroom?
Look carefully. You might spot a big clue.

Turn the page to find out what it is.

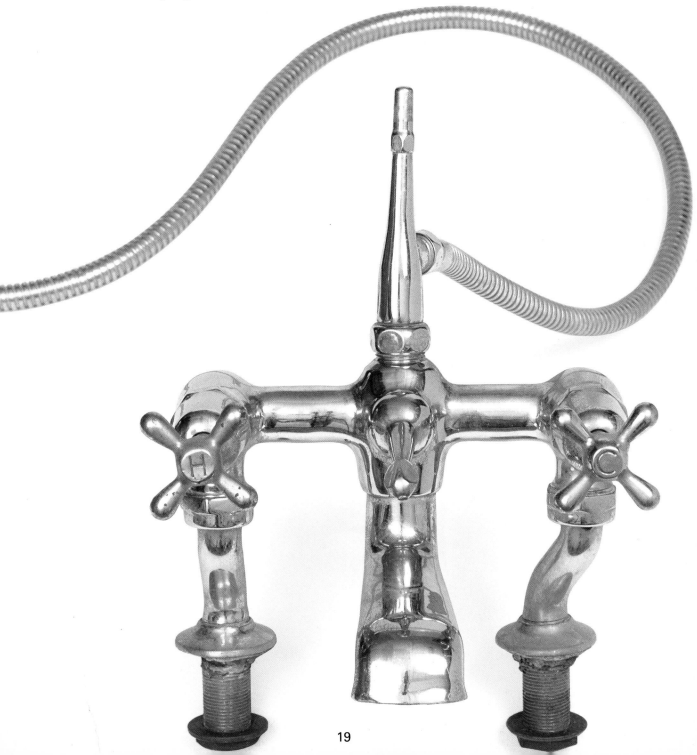

Andrew is having his hair washed.
Can you spot the mystery object?
It's a **mixer tap**.

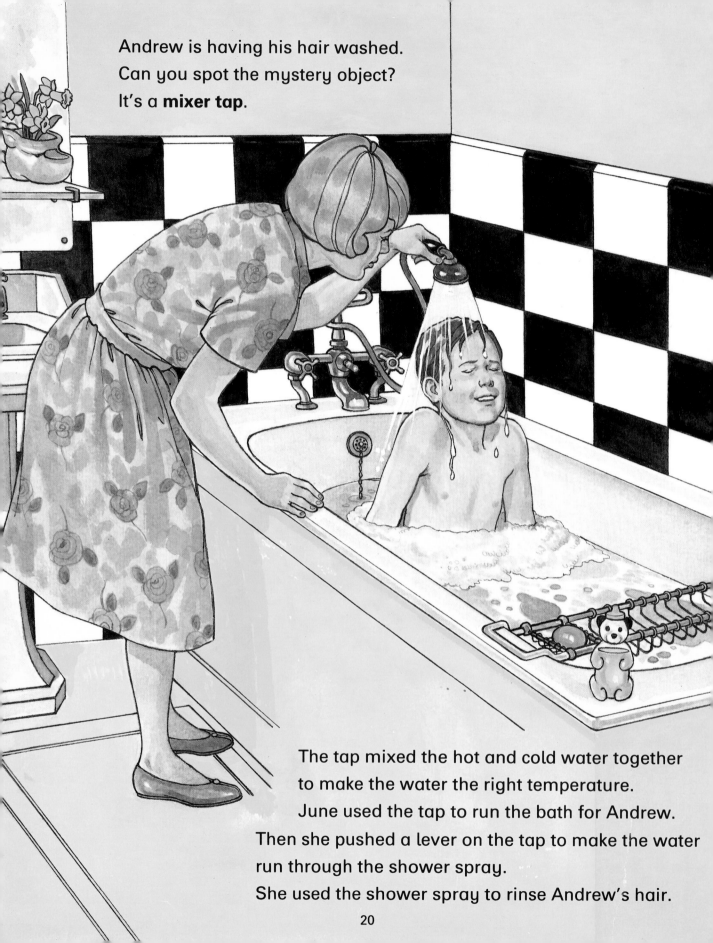

The tap mixed the hot and cold water together
to make the water the right temperature.
June used the tap to run the bath for Andrew.
Then she pushed a lever on the tap to make the water
run through the shower spray.
She used the shower spray to rinse Andrew's hair.

20

Now that you know a bit more about bathtime and washing
and how they have changed over the last hundred years,
see if you can guess what this mystery object is.
The outside is made of wood
and it has a handle at one end.
Look closely.
The writing will give you
a big clue.

You will find the answer on page 24.

Time-Line

These pages show you the objects in this book and the objects which we find in bathrooms nowadays.

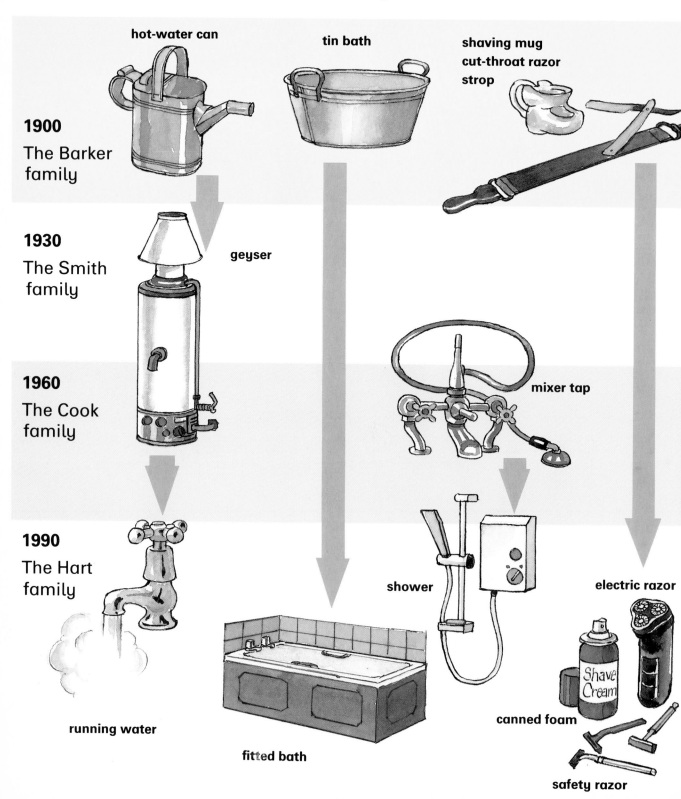

hot-water can

tin bath

shaving mug
cut-throat razor
strop

1900
The Barker family

1930
The Smith family

geyser

1960
The Cook family

mixer tap

1990
The Hart family

shower

electric razor

running water

fitted bath

canned foam

Shave Cream

safety razor

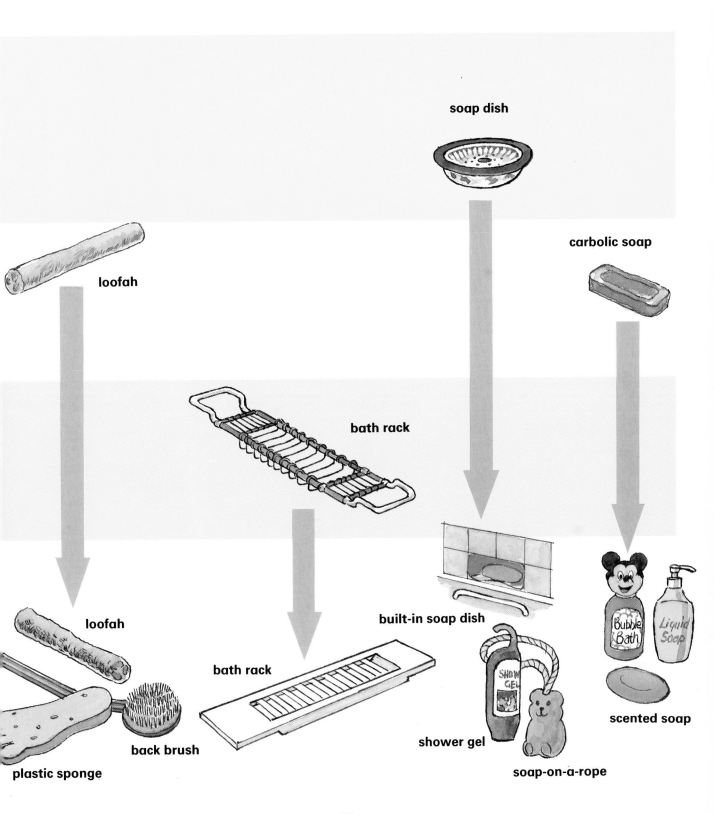

soap dish

carbolic soap

loofah

bath rack

loofah

bath rack

built-in soap dish

back brush

plastic sponge

shower gel

soap-on-a-rope

scented soap

Index

The **mystery object** on page 21 is a **thermometer**. When Lucy Barker was a child in 1900, it was used to test how hot a baby's bathwater was.

For parents and teachers

More about the objects and pictures in this book

Pages 5/6 The Barkers lived in a large industrial town. In 1900, few houses had running water. Country people collected rainwater in barrels. Town dwellers often shared a single tap per street. Portable baths were usually made from galvanised zinc. Most people bathed only once a week.

Pages 7/8 Most families bathed in the kitchen as it was the warmest room in the house. Very poor families had no kitchen range and had to wash at a cold tap or pump or visit a public bath house. Hot-water cans were made of copper and brass.

Pages 9/10 A washstand set might include a jug, bowl, potty, soap dish and toothbrush mug. Slop buckets were usually made of white china. Some people heated water and even washed in the copper.

Pages 11/12 Cut-throat razors were very dangerous. The safety razor, which had a small disposable blade inside a metal holder, was invented in 1901. The electric razor was invented in 1931.

Pages 13/14 The Smiths lived in a semi-detached house in a new town. By 1930 about 90% of town houses had running water but many country areas had none. New houses similar to the Smiths' were being built with bathrooms.

Pages 15/16 A loofah is the fibrous seed pod of a plant. Carbolic soap was designed for scrubbing floors but was widely used in poorer homes because of its disinfectant qualities and low price.

Pages 17/18 The Cooks lived in one of the new towns built in the 1960s. In spite of the availability of plastic goods, metal bath racks were very popular. Separate bathrooms, running hot water and a wide range of bathroom products made bathing a pleasure rather than a weekly chore.

Pages 19/20 Showers became increasingly popular from the 1960s onwards. Soapless shampoo was invented in 1933.

Things to do

History Mysteries will provide an excellent starting point for all kinds of history work. There are lots of general ideas which can be drawn out of the pictures, particularly in relation to the way washing, clothes, family size and lifestyles have changed in the last 100 years. Below are some starting points and ideas for follow up activities.

1 Work on families and family trees can be developed from the families on pages 2/3, bearing in mind that many children do not come from two-parent, nuclear families. Why do the families in the book have different surnames even though they are related? How have their clothes and hair styles changed over time?

2 Find out more about bathtime and washing in the past from a variety of sources, including interviews with older people in the community, books, bathroom advertisements in old magazines, museums and manufacturers' information. Bathtime and washing wasn't the same for everyone. Why not?

3 There is one object which is in one picture of the 1900s, one picture of the 1930s, and one picture of the 1960s. Can you find it?

4 Arrange a visit to a stately home or old house which has a bathroom or old bathing equipment on show.

5 Look at the differences between the photographs and the illustrations in this book. What different kinds of things can they tell you?

6 Make your own collection of bathing and washing objects or pictures. You can build up an archive or school museum over several years by encouraging children to bring in old objects, collecting unwanted items from parents, collecting from junk shops and jumble sales. You may also be able to borrow handling collections from your local museum or library service.

7 Encouraging the children to look at the objects is a useful start, but they will get more out of this if you organise some practical activities which help to develop their powers of observation. These might include drawing the objects, describing an object to another child who must then pick out the object from the collection, or writing descriptions of the objects for labels or for catalogue cards.

8 Encourage the children to answer questions. What do the objects look and feel like? What are they made of? What makes them work? How old are they? How could you find out more about them? Do they do the job they are supposed to do?

9 What do the objects tell us about the people who used them? Children might do some writing, drawing or role play, imagining themselves as the owners of different objects.

10 Children might find a mystery object in their own home or school for the others to draw, write about and identify. Children can compare the objects in the book with objects in their own home or school.

11 If you have an exhibition, try pairing old objects with their nearest modern counterparts. Talk about each pair. Some useful questions might be: How can you tell which is older? Which objects have changed most over time? Why? What do you think of the older objects? What would people have thought of them when they were new? Can you test how well the objects work? Is the modern version better than the older version?

12 Make a time-line using your objects. You might find the time-line at the back of this book useful. You could include pictures in your time-line and other markers to help the children gain a sense of chronology. Use your time-line to bring out the elements of *change* (eg. the gradual development of special rooms used as bathrooms, piped running water, en suite bathrooms, showers, electric razors, advertising, supermarkets) and *continuity* (eg. basic similarities in the process of washing, and the need for washing to stay healthy).

History Mysteries

First published 1993
A & C Black (Publishers) Limited
35 Bedford Row, London WC1R 4JH

ISBN 0-7136-3687-4

© 1993 A & C Black (Publishers) Limited

A CIP catalogue record for this book is available
from the British Library.

Acknowledgements

The authors and publishers would like to thank Mrs Tanner's Tangible History,
Suella Postles and the staff of Brewhouse Yard Museum, Nottingham,
Rita Lee, Bob and John Collingwood, and Madeline Moulton.

Photographs by Maggie Murray except for: p 4 (top) National Museum of
Photography Film & Television, Bradford; p 4 (bottom) Judy Harrison,
Format Photographers.

Filmset by Rowland Phototypesetting Limited, Bury St Edmunds, Suffolk
Printed and bound in Italy by L.E.G.O.

THE US NAVY TODAY

THE
US NAVY
TODAY

THOMAS YORK

GALLERY BOOKS
An imprint of W.H. Smith Publishers Inc.
112 Madison Avenue
New York, New York 10016

A Bison Book

Published by Gallery Books
A Division of W H Smith Publishers Inc.
112 Madison Avenue
New York, New York 10016

Produced by
Bison Books Corp.
17 Sherwood Place
Greenwich, CT 06830

ISBN 0-8317-9078-4

Printed in Hong Kong

1 2 3 4 5 6 7 8 9 10

Picture Credits

Boeing Marine Systems: 4-5, 74 top and
  bottom
PHAN Eslinger/PHAN Langway,
  US Navy: 91 top
PH2 Robert S Escue, US Navy: 88 top
PH3 D A Fort, US Navy: 39
PH1 Ron Garrison, US Navy: 86 top
General Dynamics Co: 70-71, 72-73
PH1 Harold J Gerwien, US Navy: 20
JOC James R Giusti, US Navy: 32 top
PH1/AC R H Green, US Navy: 32
Grumman Aircraft Co: 28-29, 89
PH2 Robert Hamilton, US Navy: 12-13
JOCS Kirby Harrison, US Navy: 41 bottom
PH1 Jeff Hilton US Navy: 22, 55 top
PHC William E Kendall US Navy: 64 bottom
JO1 Lewis, US Navy: 17
PH2 David B Loveall, US Navy: 87 bottom
McDonnell Douglas Corp: 43 top, 65, 74-75
PH1 Terry C Mitchell, US Navy: 18 all, 19
PHC Ron Oliver, US Navy: 21
PH3 T Olsen /PHAN M Langway,
  US Navy: 32 bottom
PH2 A E Rochells, US Navy: 30 top
PH3 Lee Schnell, US Navy: 34-35, 87 top
PH2 Rick Sforza, US Navy: 1, 50-51, 84,
  92-93
PH2 D Smith, US Navy: 55 bottom
Perry Thorsvik, US Navy: 43 bottom
United States Department of Defense: 27
  right, 58-59, 62-63, 69, 83 top, 99
United States Navy: 7, 11, 25, 26-27, 28 left,
  30-31, 35 both, 38 both, 40, 41 top, 42, 44-45,
  56 left, 56-57, 58 top, 62 top, 64 top, 68 both,
  73 top, 81 bottom, 88 bottom
W M Welch, US Navy: 30 bottom
PH1 Wood, US Navy: 16
© **Bill Yenne:** 2-3, 6, 8-9, 10, 14-15, 23, 24, 36-
  37, 46-47, 47, 48, 49, 54, 54-55, 60-61, 66-67,
  78-79, 80, 81 top, 82-83, 85, 86 bottom, 90-91,
  94-95

Page 1: This PO 2d Class, sporting a badge with 'crow,' chevrons and his specialty rating, was photographed by PH2 Rick Sforza.

Page 2-3: The USS *New Jersey* (BB 62) in San Francisco Bay during the celebration of the 40th anniversary of the end of World War II.

Below: The USS *Hercules* (PHM 2) hydrofoil, heavily armed with eight Harpoon missiles and a 76mm gun, has a speed of over 40 knots when foilborne and a range of over 1200 nautical miles if hullborne. This ship and its *Pegasus*-class sisters have faced controversy because, for all their speed and maneuverability, they are extremely expensive to build for their size and range.

Acknowledgements

The editors wish to thank the following people for supplying many of the photographs included in this book: Robert A Carlisle, head of the still photo branch of the Department of the Navy's Office of Information, and PH2 Rick Sforza, ship's photographer from the USS *New Jersey*.

Edited by Carolyn Soto and Deirdre Levenson

Designed by Bill Yenne

CONTENTS

INTRODUCTION TO THE UNITED STATES NAVY

'Our status as a free society and world power is not based on brute strength. When we have taken up arms, it has been for the defense of freedom for ourselves and for other peaceful nations who needed our help. But now, faced with the development of weapons with immense destructive power, we have no choice but to maintain ready defense forces that are second to none. Yes, the cost is high — but the cost of neglect would be infinitely higher.'

(President Ronald Reagan at the recommissioning of the USS *New Jersey* on 28 December 1982 at the Long Beach, California, Naval Shipyard.)

The United States Navy today is the largest and most powerful armed force on the high seas. Established more than 200 years ago to protect the maritime interests of the 13 American colonies, it remains a critical component of the nation's defense strategy. Its advanced fleet power of 37 nuclear-powered ballistic missile submarines (SSBN), unique undersea vessels developed and pioneered by Navy, is the maritime leg of the the US nuclear defense triad that includes

The Navy looks to tomorrow. Seamen aboard the USS *New Jersey* (BB 62) *(opposite)* and the sailor with a sextant *(above)* can look forward to manning warships fitted with the most modern of weapons.

long-range bombers and intercontinental ballistic missiles (ICBM). The US Navy also boasts the fourth largest air force in the world, with more than 6000 fighters, support aircraft and helicopters in its inventory. The only challenger on the high seas is the Soviet blue-water navy, a growing menace to US naval supremacy around the globe.

It is a navy in transition. Neglected during the Vietnam era of the 1960s and allowed to decline in the 1970s, the Navy is experiencing renewed attention in the 1980s. Billions of dollars are being spent to build dozens of new ships for the fleet. At the beginning of the decade, there were just over 450 ships in the Navy, compared to a World War II high of about 2500. The present number is about 550. The goal is to deploy 600 ships at the end of the decade.

The Navy today is a flexible and sophisticated armed force designed to protect and defend the United States at sea. The major portion of the surface fleet is divided into battle groups structured around the Navy's 13 deployable aircraft carriers. These include four of the largest warships in the world — one *Enterprise*-class and

The flags are out for a port call to San Francisco aboard the USS *New Jersey* (BB 62). Its 16-inch guns saw action in WW II and Vietnam, but the ship was 'mothballed' until its recommissioning in 1982. This *Iowa*-class battleship can serve as an integrated part of a Carrier Battle Group, spearhead assault force or lead its own Surface Action Group.

three *Nimitz*-class carriers. These carriers are supported and protected by a fleet of battleships, cruisers, destroyers, frigates and submarines. Many of them are nuclear powered.

The battleships are an unusual feature of the modern Navy. Once believed to be obsolete, the World War II-era *Iowa*-class batleships have been reactivated and rearmed with advanced armament and antimissile defense systems. Three battleships, the USS *New Jersey* (BB 62), the USS *Iowa* (BB 61) and the USS *Missouri* (BB 63) have already been recommissioned. A fourth, the USS *Wisconsin* (BB 64), is scheduled to be brought out of mothballs and recommissioned by the end of the decade. The very high accuracy of their 16-inch guns and the lethal effect of the massive projectiles make the *Iowas* four of the most effective conventional fighting ships in the world today.

The other warships of the fleet are fitted with the latest in defense technology and weaponry on the high seas. Vessels with advanced electronic countermeasure and missile defense systems include the *Ticonderoga*-class cruisers. They are armed with the computerized Aegis air-defense system, which can direct and control up to 18 ship-to-air missiles against high-density air attacks from Soviet anti-ship cruise missiles.

Sophisticated *Spruance*- and *Kidd*-class destroyers and the sleek *Oliver Hazard Perry*-class frigates also contribute to making the US Navy the most advanced in the world. Dozens of other warships and support ships play prominent roles. Among them are amphibious-warfare ships and helicopter-landingcraft carriers, as well as numerous support vessels from mobile logistic ships to under way replenishment ships.

In addition to the ships of the fleet, nearly 2500 fighters and attack aircraft and their weapons systems are on duty and ready for action. These include the A-6E Intruder all-weather carrier-based attack planes and the new F/A-18 Hornet multirole tactical aircraft. The Navy's versatile F-14 Tomcat fighters are armed with Phoenix missiles effective at ranges up to 100 miles. Other weapons systems include the Harpoon air or surface-to-surface missiles, Tomahawk tactical antiship and land-attack missiles, acoustic-honing antisubmarine-warfare (ASW) torpedoes and attack and ASW shipborne helicopters.

Officers welcome Vice President George Bush aboard the USS *Enterprise* (CVN 65) on a beautiful August 1985 day. On any day, however, their distinguished visitor would find the ship in top maintenance. The weapons department seaman *(opposite)* spruces up an anchor with practical rust preventive paint.

ORGANIZATION AND STRUCTURE OF THE UNITED STATES NAVY

The US Navy was established on 13 October 1775 when the Continental Congress enacted legislation that created the Continental Navy of the American Revolution. Later, following ratification of the Constitution, the Department of the Navy and the office of the secretary of the Navy were established by an act of Congress on 30 April 1798.

The Department of the Navy is one of three military departments—Army, Navy and Air Force—in the Department of Defense. Each is headed by executive department secretaries, who do not have cabinet rank. The secretary of the Navy, who is responsible for the Navy's overall readiness, has his office, like those of the other secretaries, at the Pentagon, in Arlington, Virginia, just a few miles from the White House. The secretary has several aides, including a civilian undersecretary, a deputy undersecretary and various assistants. The chief of naval operations is an admiral and the secretary's principal naval advisor. He commands personnel within the Navy and Marine Corps as directed by the secretary.

The Department of the Navy is divided into three major components: the Navy Department, the Operating Forces and the Shore Establishment. The Navy Department comprises the central offices and bureaus of the executive arm of the Department of the Navy which are located in Washington, DC.

The Operating Forces include sea commands such as the Atlantic Fleet, headquartered at Norfolk Naval Base, Virginia; the Pacific Fleet, headquartered at Pearl Harbor Naval Base, Hawaii; and US Naval Forces, Europe, headquartered in London, England. The Pacific Fleet consists of the Third and Seventh Fleets. The Second Fleet is assigned to the Atlantic Fleet and the Sixth Fleet is assigned to the US Naval Forces, Europe. Each of these smaller, numbered fleets defends a separate geographic area.

The Second Fleet operates in the western Atlantic Ocean, with Norfolk, Virginia the home port of the flagship.

The Sixth Fleet operates in the Mediterranean Sea, with Gaeta, Italy the home port of the flagship.

The Third Fleet operates in the middle and eastern Pacific Ocean, with Pearl Harbor, Hawaii the home port of the flagship.

The Seventh Fleet operates in the western Pacific Ocean, with Yokosuka, Japan the home port of the flagship.

The numbered fleets are divided into task forces. Organization of these forces is flexible, depending upon the requirements of the Navy. The commanders in chief of the major fleets direct the several subordinate commanders who control various types of groups and forces. Generally, each subordinate commander has control of a single type of ship, such as submarines, and is handed responsibility for developing tactics and doctrine as well as providing manpower, spare parts and safety standards to the fleet. The naval reserve force is responsible for the organization, training and mobilization of reserve ships, aircraft and personnel.

Two additional major naval operating forces are the Military Sealift Command (MSC) and the Naval Reserve Force. The MSC is operated by the Navy for all services and consists of ships manned by civilian government employees and commercial ships employed on a contract basis. The ships are used to transport service personnel and their dependents, combat troops, supplies and materiel to all parts of the globe.

The Shore Establishment provides support to the fleets and other operating forces by training personnel as well as supplying and maintaining material and equipment. It includes naval districts, naval bases, ammunition depots, hospitals, training commands, communications and intelligence.

The Shore Establishment consists of various commands, including the Bureau of Naval Personnel, Naval Medical Command, Naval Oceanography Command, Naval Space Command, Naval Legal Service Command, Naval Telecommunications Command, Naval Intelligence Command, Naval Investigative Service, Naval Education and Training Command and Civilian Personnel Command.

The Bureau of Naval Personnel plans and directs the procurement, distribution, administration, and career development of Navy active duty and reserve personnel, while the Naval Medical Command directs the provision of medical and dental services for the Navy and Marine Corps.

The Naval Oceanography Command is a functional field command coordinated by the commander of Naval Oceanography and the superintendent of the US Naval Observatory. Its programs cover the science, technology, engineering and operations essential to exploring the ocean and the atmosphere and to providing astronomical information and time estimates for naval operations. The Naval Oceanographic Program, for instance, is responsible for the physical sciences of hydrography. It collects data for the charting of the oceans and establishes geodetic references for navigation. This program also studies underwater acoustics, water dynamics and corrosion, as well as meteorology and astronomy. These studies are used to calculate precise geodetic positions on the globe and to establish the precise time of day required for navigation.

The Naval Space Command oper-

The Midshipman Drum & Bugle Corps in spiffy dress and polished brass perform during the commissioning of the nuclear-powered strategic missile submarine USS *Ohio* (SSBN 726) on 11 November 1981.

Although the decks may not always be made of teak (as they are on this battleship), swabbing them will always be part of the regimen of daily life for Navy seamen.

ates space systems, such as satellites, to support US forces worldwide, while the Naval Legal Service Command administers legal services programs. Naval Telecommunications is responsible for telecommunications systems, while Naval Intelligence is responsible for security and intelligence gathering. The Naval Investigative Service commands law enforcement, criminal investigative and counterintelligence support. Naval Information Systems is responsible for the administration and coordination of computer data information systems, while the Civilian Personnel Command oversees the management of the 350,000 civilian employees of the Navy. Naval Education and Training provides shore-based education and training.

TRAINING AND EDUCATION OF NAVY PERSONNEL

The Navy's mission is to remain ready to conduct operations at sea in support of US political and military interests close to home waters and abroad. This responsibility is carried on the shoulders of its 565,000 men and women, in conjunction with the support of the US Marines. The sophisticated ships, submarines and aircraft of the Navy call for highly skilled and trained individuals. In fact, in recent years more than 90 percent of the Navy's new recruits have earned high school diplomas before joining the service. To prepare the thousands

of men and women for their tasks, the Navy has established dozens of schools and training programs ranging from basic training to PhD programs affiliated with major colleges and universities.

The premier educational facility for the Navy is the US Naval Academy at Annapolis, Maryland. Founded in 1845 as the Naval School, the academy today admits 1200 men and women each year, most of them from high schools across the nation. The academy offers 18 majors in the subjects of engineering, science and math. Upon graduation, each midshipman receives a bachelor of science degree and then undertakes at least five years of service in return for the privilege of getting a college education. Each candidate must obtain a nomination from any of several possible sources, including nominations from US congressional representatives in the district where the applying candidate lives. The candidate must also qualify scholastically, medically and physically.

The Navy also administers a Naval Reserve Officers Training Corps program in more than 63 colleges and universities throughout the nation. About 1400 officers are commissioned annually in these programs. In addition, the Navy operates postgraduate schools for masters and doctoral pro-

A Navy color guard and drill team trains long hours for its performance (below), and the recruits (opposite) listen to long hours of indoctrination lectures about the Navy.

grams, with 800 graduates receiving degrees each year. It participates in graduate programs in more than 50 schools across the nation, including such prestigious schools and universities as Harvard University, The Massachusetts Institute of Technology, The University of California and Stanford University. Some 400 degrees are conferred in these programs, in subject areas ranging from religion to nuclear physics. A professional war college, staff college, and medical school are also operated by the Navy.

It is possible for enlisted personnel to advance to the officer's rank by successfully completing the proper educational programs in the service. Below the officer ranks, the Navy offers a two-year, associate-degree-granting program for about 2500 enlisted men and women annually through participating colleges and universities. An enlisted commissioning program annually gives degrees to about 200 sailors who have two years of college education in the sciences or arts.

In addition to basic training for all enlisted personnel, the Navy offers several advanced training schools. There are dozens of these schools located at bases and training facilities throughout the Navy.

There are 565,000 men and women in the US Navy. All are volunteers since the US military no longer uses the draft to supply its manpower needs.

While the great majority of the Navy's personnel consists of men, many stationed on warships, an in-

This page: Recruits aboard the training destroyer USS *Recruit* (TDE 1) get instructions and then try them out. Here they practice mooring, but they will also learn anchoring, block and tackle, and other basic seamanship skills.

creasing number of women are taking up important roles at shore facilities and on selected ships in the modern Navy. Women are forbidden by federal mandate from serving on warships, but they are allowed to serve on support ships such as submarine tenders, oilers and supply ships. There are more than 41,000 women in the enlisted ranks, or 8.5 percent of the total number of people in the enlisted ranks, while there are more than 6600 women serving in the officers' ranks, or 9.6 percent of the total number. Although they are restricted from combat roles, there are no barriers to education or advancement in the Navy. Women can be found at all levels, from basic recruits to admirals. Women serve in such roles as public relations officers, administrators and instructors.

Twelve percent of the Navy's sailors and officers are black Americans, while more than 3 percent are Hispanic Americans. Other minorities

account for nearly 6 percent of the total for both officers and sailors.

SHIPBOARD ORGANIZATION

US Navy ships are supplied with enough officers and enlisted personnel of various grades and ranks to operate and fight efficiently. Ships are organized for war, with the idea that crew assignments can be changed or expanded quickly when conditions warrant. Such organization is based on a grouping of functions and personnel intended to minimize duplication or overlap of command responsibilities.

Any officer in command of a ship, regardless of rank, is called the captain, but he is known as the commanding officer (CO). Based on centuries of tradition, his authority is absolute, within bounds of the Navy regulations. The CO is totally responsible for the operation, safety and appearance of

the ship he commands, as well as the health, morale, and welfare of his crew. Other responsibilities include the safe navigation of the ship, condition and appearance of materiel and personnel, proper stationing of trained lookouts and preparation of the ship for battle. The CO may delegate these responsibilities, but delegation does not relieve him of the responsibility for the ship.

During combat, the CO is required to engage the enemy and fight to the best of the ship's ability, and he must not disengage the ship until the fighting is completed. The commanding officer's battle station is that station where the action can be best fought. In case of the loss of the ship, both custom and regulations require that the CO assure that abandon-ship procedures are completed. All personnel should be off the ship before the CO abandons ship himself.

The executive officer (XO) is the next in the chain of command aboard ship. If the CO is absent, disabled,

Above: **Recruits receive training on various exterior parts of an aircraft. The over 565,000 personnel in the Navy started at this point at one time.**

relieved from duty, or detached without relief, the XO assumes command. He is also responsible for helping to maintain the general efficiency of the ship. With the assistance of the heads of the departments, he arranges and coordinates all of the work, drills, exercises, personnel organization, and the policing and inspection of the ship.

Assisting the XO are several assistants, such as the personnel officer, the training officer, the educational services officer, the substance abuse coordinator, and the command master chief.

Each ship in the Navy follows a standardized organization divided into departments, with the number of departments included in a shipboard organization dependent on the type and size of the ship. Departments are grouped together as either command

or support departments. In most cases, an officer heading a command department is a line officer eligible to exercise command in the event of the loss of superior officers. In aircraft carriers, the operations and air departments are headed by naval aviators.

Warships with ordnance, such as gun batteries, torpedoes, missiles, etc, have a weapons department headed by a weapons officer. Some surface warships with combat systems and some classes of submarines have combat-systems departments headed by combat systems officers. Ships not dependent on ordnance have deck departments usually commanded by first lieutenants. Aircraft carriers and some other ships have a weapons or combat-systems department in addition to a deck department. Under the weapons or combat-systems officers, the department is responsible for the operation, care and maintenance of the ship's armament and weapon-fire-control systems.

Above: **Enlisted men aboard a tank-landing ship on bridge watch.**

Right: **LCDR Lukinbeal serving as officer on deck on the bridge of his vessel.**

The weapons department operates the guns, torpedoes, fire-control systems and sonar. This department also keeps the ship's side and other exterior surfaces painted and clean. The deck hands of the weapons department are experienced in block and tackle, anchoring and mooring, running the ship's boats and other chores of seamanship. Gunner's mates and fire-control technicians are responsible for arming and firing the guns and tracking and killing submarines.

The operations department handles such communication functions as electronic warfare and intelligence gathering from the radar and radio systems. The information is collected, displayed and passed along to those who are responsible for guiding and fighting the ship. Its electronics tech-

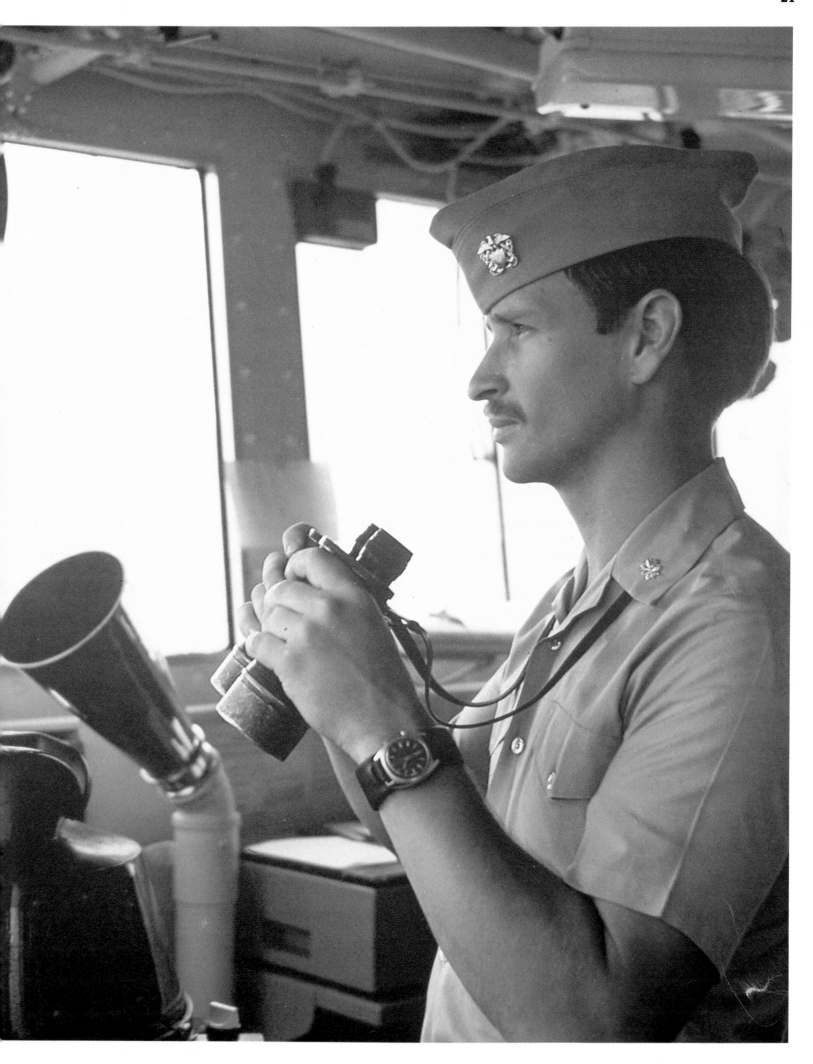

nicians operate and maintain the electronic equipment. Radarmen operate the air- and surface-search radars. Quartermasters and signalmen are responsible for visual communication on the bridge.

The engineering department runs the engine plants that provide power to the ship and furnish electricity for the guns, radar, radios, air conditioning, and other auxiliary machinery. The engineering officer may be assigned several assistants, such as the main-propulsion assistant, damage-control assistant, and the electrical officer.

The supply department is responsible for feeding and clothing aboard ship. The galley, mess hall and general storerooms are operated by cooks, bakers, commissarymen and storekeepers. Disbursing clerks maintain pay records. The supply officer operates the laundry, ship's store, fountain, and barber shop.

The medical department is responsible for maintaining the health of personnel of the command, and routinely inspects the ship's food service, as well as living, berthing, and working spaces to make sure they are sanitary. The dental department is responsible for the dental care and oral health of the ship's personnel.

Navy aircraft-squadron organization differs from shipboard organization, with each squadron divided into an administrative department and a safety department. Most also have operational and maintenance departments. The administrative department handles all administrative chores within the squadron, such as official correspondence, personnel records and directives, while the safety department is responsible for all matters concerning the squadron safety program. The operational department is responsible for the operational readiness and efficiency of the squadron. The maintenance department maintains the aircraft. Combined, the squadrons assigned to each ship form a wing.

The division is the basic unit of the shipboard organization, and ship divisions are divided into watches or sections. The number of divisions in a department varies among ships, and the number of personnel in a division may be only a few or as many as 200.

Required aboard each ship are such documents as a standard organization and regulations manual, a battle organization manual, and a watch

Above: **Crewmen sweep down the helicopter deck of the battleship USS *Iowa* (BB 61).**

Opposite: **Taking weather readings is but one of the many operations within the Naval Oceanography Command.**

and station bill to ensure a well-coordinated team. These documents outline in detail for each ship the assignment of officers and enlisted personnel.

Ships are operated according to conditions of readiness or alerts, ranging between Condition Watch I, the maximum state of readiness when crews have been sent to battle stations prepared for fighting, and Condition Watch V, when the ship is in port. Each ship has a battle bill—the organized plan for action against the enemy. It lists the stations that must be manned under battle conditions and shows personnel requirements for manning those stations. These assignments are made according to billet numbers, rather than individuals. Division officers take into account personal qualifications, then assign crew members to billets and enter their names on the divisions' watch, quarter and station bills.

Aboard ship, security watches are stood to prevent sabotage, to protect property from damage or theft, to prevent access to restricted areas and to protect personnel. Included in the watches are sentry duty, barracks watches, fire watches and watches stood under way. The watch system is divided into two parts, when the ship is in port and when it is under way. Key assignments include the command duty officer, the officer of the deck, jun-

ior officer of the deck, junior officer of the watch and combat information center watch officer.

A ship's deck log is a daily record, by watches, of activity aboard the ship—events and occurrences that concern the crew and the safety of the ship. The ship's navigator is responsible for keeping the log. Accuracy is very important, because such entries often constitute important legal evidence in judicial and administrative fact-finding proceedings for incidents involving the ship and its crew. Information in the log includes such facts as the ship's operating orders, its courses and speeds, positions, state of the sea and weather, damage to the ship or its cargo, deaths or injuries to personnel, records of meeting or courts-martial and other formal boards, as well as changes in ship personnel or passengers. An engineering log is also kept pertaining to the important events and data of the propulsion plant.

The space provided for the officers' living quarters usually is located near the wardroom. This is the part of the ship known as 'officers' country.' If there is room, senior officers are assigned individual staterooms. Junior officers and warrant officers usually share staterooms or are assigned to a bunkroom, while petty officers are bunked in large compartments containing tiered bunks and metal lockers.

Eating aboard ship is divided by rank. On flagships there are usually six messes. The flag mess is held for the admiral, while the captain's mess is for the captain. The mess in the wardroom is held for the other officers, except warrant officers who eat with the chief petty officers. The general enlisted mess is held for all enlisted personnel except for chief petty officers. Enlisted men are given their food by the government; officers must pay for their food since they are paid a subsistence allowance to cover the cost of meals. On small ships, messes are combined.

Ships of the US Navy are usually divided into three classes: combatants, auxiliaries and service crafts. The bulk of combatants are warships, ranging from the mighty nuclear-powered aircraft carriers to fleet-patrol ships. Auxiliary ships include oilers, ammunitions ships and store ships, as well as tenders, transports, cargo ships, repair ships and salvage ships. Service ships range from harbor tugs to floating derricks and dry docks.

THE FLEET OF THE UNITED STATES NAVY

DEPLOYMENT

The United States has become increasingly dependent upon trade with its friends and allies since the end of the Second World War. Ninety percent of all international trade is carried by ship. With so much of this international trade carried across vital sea lanes, maritime strategy has become critical to the United States. Protection of the sea lanes is a major reason Navy warships are deployed so far from home ports. The Navy has the responsibility of deterring attacks on the US from the sea and ensuring unimpeded use of ocean trade routes in times of hostility. This responsibility has spurred the Navy to maintain equality with the Soviet navy—its principal potential opponent. The Soviets have deployed increasing numbers of warships and submarines throughout the major oceans of the world.

In the Pacific, Soviet ships could threaten at any time to cut off the flow of material and supplies from America's trading partners in the Far East such as Japan, Taiwan and Hong Kong. They also could threaten to sever the flow of oil carried by ship from the

Opposite: **The awesome striking power of 16-inch guns aboard this Navy battleship protects the carrier in the background, the USS *Enterprise* (CVN 65).**

Above: **An F-14 Tomcat from the 'Jolly Rogers' squadron aboard the carrier USS *Nimitz* (CVN 68) makes a low-altitude turn above two nuclear-powered guided missile cruisers under way. The F-14 protects the fleet from air attack.**

Alaskan oil fields to the continental United States.

In the Atlantic Ocean, the Soviet navy poses an ever-present threat to the United States and its allies of the North Atlantic Treaty Organization (NATO). During 1984, in the waters of the Barents, Norwegian and North Seas, the Soviet navy held the largest exercises ever conducted in Europe. More that 200 ships participated, not including more than 70 submarines, which pose a vital threat to shipping and surface ships in the event of hostilities. The Soviet Union now has more than 270 attack submarines in her fleet. In 1942, during World War II, Germany almost shut down the Allied flow of materials and supplies across the Atlantic with fewer than 60 submarines. The US Navy currently has about 200 active surface-combatant ships and 100 active submarines in its fleet.

To guard US interests on the high seas, the Navy maintains a high degree of readiness for action in regions where combat could be expected in time of war, such as the Mediterranean Sea and the Indian Ocean. Typically, two carrier groups are stationed in the Mediterranean and two in the

Below: An aerial port quarter view of the battleship USS *New Jersey* (BB 62)—at upper left—under way with ships assigned to her Central American task group: a fleet oiler *(top center)*, a cruiser *(far left)*, and frigates including the USS *Knox* (FF 1052) *(lower left)*.

Below right: The USS *Mars* (AFS 1) combat store ship carries two CH-46 Sea Knight helicopters and is armed with four 3-inch/50 caliber guns. Most of the seven *Mars*-class ships are less than 20 years old and in excellent condition to respond to additional requirements placed on the Navy's auxiliary forces.

western Pacific. They are backed by carrier groups and other support ships based at ports in the United States. Other surface groups are deployed at strategic stations throughout the world.

Navy surface ships are usually organized around carriers, amphibious or replenishment ships, with the number of defending battleships, cruisers, destroyers, and frigates greatly exceeding the number of ships being protected. For instance, 20 to 30 combatant ships are often grouped together to provide cover to unarmed landing ships as they are moved to landing areas under hostile conditions. The same number can be expected to escort replenishment ships to forward areas to keep fighting ships on station in times of hostilities. Other ships would be needed to protect convoys carrying troops, supplies and materials. Some of these defense responsibilities are handled by attack submarines, which would be responsible for antisubmarine warfare (ASW) duties during hostilities. Up to three submarines are assigned to each task group constructed around a carrier.

Others are assigned the duties of protecting the larger and more vulnerable Poseidon and Trident submarines as they patrol waters far from their home bases.

CARRIERS

The first carrier specifically designed to carry and launch aircraft joined the US Navy in 1934. However, the importance of the carrier to modern naval warfare was not established until World War II when the Japanese ably proved the capability of the carrier-launched air attack at Pearl Harbor on 7 December 1941. Aircraft from the carriers sank or severely damaged a number of major US warships lying at anchor in the harbor. In the naval actions that followed in the Pacific Ocean, US carriers became the critical instruments of war in establishing military superiority over the Japanese. But as carriers developed in size and capability in the postwar era, they became controversial and their futures were challenged. In spite of the fact that carriers have been called upon dozens of times to successfully carry out military actions since the end of World War II, opposition to them has been loud. Opponents argue that they are too costly to construct and lack adequate defenses. They say thay are vulnerable to both nuclear and conventional weapon attacks. Despite this debate, the carriers of the US Navy remain the principal military force on

The flight deck crew *(above)* of the nuclear-powered carrier USS *Carl Vinson* (CVN 70); and four F-14 Tomcats *(right)* over the carrier USS *John F. Kennedy* (CV 67), which is conventionally powered.

**Work aboard carriers includes mainte-
nance on an A-7 Corsair II** *(above)* **on the
USS** *Midway* **(CV 41) and monitoring
gauges in the machine room** *(below)* **on
the USS** *America* **(CV 66).**

Right: **An 'easy' catapult launch of an
F-14 flying 'hands off.'**

Opposite below: **The USS** *Nimitz* **carries
some of its 90 aircraft on deck.**

the high seas and will remain so well
into the next century. All US carriers
constructed since 1964 have been
nuclear powered.

The backbone of the Navy fleet are
the nuclear-powered carriers, with the
six carriers of the *Nimitz*-class among
the largest warships in the world
today. Four are currently deployable:
they are the USS *Nimitz* (CVN 68), the
USS *Dwight D Eisenhower* (CVN 69),
the USS *Carl Vinson* (CVN 70) and the
USS *Theodore Roosevelt* (CVN 71).
Each has an overall length of 1092 feet
and deck width of 252 feet and they

each displace over 93,000 tons when fully loaded with aircraft. Each ship can steam up to 33 knots with power supplied by two large nuclear reactors and four sets of turbines. They carry more than 90 aircraft and helicopter, many of them equipped to deliver nuclear attack weapons. In spite of the awesome fire power of the squadrons aboard the carriers, defenses are minimal. Along with the other US carriers, the *Nimitz*-class carriers are lightly armed, fitted with three Phalanx close-in weapons systems, Sea Sparrow missiles and 20mm antiaircraft guns

Carrier flight deck operations can include arming a 250-lb bomb *(above)*; launching aircraft from the deck *(below)*; and stand-ing ready during vertical replenishment operations by a CH-46 Sea Knight helicop-ter *(opposite)*.

as their only defense. They rely on their fighter aircraft and attack bombers for long-range protection.

Two more carriers in this class are under construction or planned: the USS *Abraham Lincoln*, expected to join the fleet in 1989, and the USS *George Washington*, expected to join the fleet in 1991 and replace the USS *Coral Sea*. These are expected to be the last carriers, large or small, to be funded and constructed for some years to come by the United States. Many Congressmen are reluctant to fund more of them because they be-lieve the massive ships can be easily immobilized and sunk. The comple-ment of men on the *Nimitz*-class carri-ers is 3300, with another 3000 in the air wing on board.

The one ship of the nuclear-powered *Enterprise* class, the USS *Enterprise* (CVN 65), is slightly smaller than the *Nimitz*-class carriers. Displacing 89,600 tons fully loaded, she was con-structed with eight nuclear power plants, rather than four, for propul-

After World War II carriers became the most important ships in the fleet. The Indian Ocean Task Force *(below)* from back to front: the USS *Nimitz* (CVN 68), USS *Midway* (CV 41) and USS *Kitty Hawk* (CV 63); the USS *Ranger* (CV 61) *(bottom right)*; the maintenance crew working on an F-4 Phantom on deck *(top right)*; and the superstructure of the USS *Coral Sea* (CV 43) *(overleaf)*.

sion. The first large nuclear-powered surface warship constructed, she was commissioned in late 1961. Like the *Nimitz*-class designs, she carries more than 80 aircraft and helicopters. She carries a complement of 3100 men and 2400 in the air wing.

The single carrier USS *John F Kennedy* (CV 67) of the *John F Kennedy* class was originally intended to be nuclear powered. However, she was laid down with a conventional power plant because of a debate in Congress over the cost of nuclear warships in the 1960s. She displaces 82,000 tons fully loaded, and carries approximately 85 aircraft. There are 3100 men in the ship's company and 2400 in the air wing.

The USS *John F Kennedy* closely resembles the carriers of the *Kitty Hawk* class: the USS *Kitty Hawk* (CV 63), the USS *Constellation* (CV 64) and the USS *America* (CV 66). They, in turn, closely resemble the ships of the older *Forrestal* class: the USS *Forrestal* (CV 59), the USS *Saratoga* (CV 60) and the USS *Ranger* (CV 61). All of these ships were constructed in the 1950s and 1960s. The *Kitty Hawk*-class ships displace 80,800 tons fully loaded and carry 85 aircraft, while the *Forrestal*-class carriers displace 75,900

to 79,300 tons and carry approximately 70 aircraft. Both classes have a ship's company of 2800 men and 2150 in the air wing. All are armed with Sea Sparrow missiles and the Phalanx close-in weapons system.

The *Forrestals* were the first carriers to be constructed after World War II in the years between 1952 and 1959 and they were the first to have angled decks—a British invention. The USS *Forrestal* was the first carrier designed to handle jet aircraft from its decks.

All of the older carriers in the fleet have been updated and improved or in some cases completely overhauled. Designs of the newer generation of carriers have taken advantage of the lessons learned in operating the older carriers. For example, operational weaknesses of the *Forrestals* were corrected in the *Kitty Hawks*, most nota-

bly the location the deck lifts. These were constructed at the forward end of the angled deck in the *Forrestal* class. This position interferes with the launching and landing of the aircraft. Beginning with the USS *Kitty Hawk*, all US carriers have been constucted with a port deck lift moved aft to a point where it no longer encroaches on the angled deck. The carriers can launch and recover many aircraft without the lifts hindering deck operations.

The World War II-era *Midway*-class carriers, the USS *Midway* (CV 41) and the USS *Coral Sea* (CV 43), are the smallest and oldest carriers in the fleet, displacing just 64,000 tons with a full contingent of 75 aircraft on board. Other ships constructed in this class have been retired or used for aviation training. They were the first modern warships that could not pass through the Panama Canal because of their wide size. Originally constructed with straight decks of pre-war design, they have since been modernized so that they now have angled decks and advanced radar and large deck-edge lifts. The complement of men on the

Carrier personnel can truly see the world. The USS *Enterprise* (CVN 65) sails near a tiny fishing boat in the Philippines *(opposite)*; and the USS *Nimitz* (CVN 68) views the beckoning lights of Monte Carlo *(above)*. Yet the sailor *(below)* would probably agree there's 'no place like home.'

USS *Midway* and USS *Coral Sea* is about 2700, with 1800 in the air wing.

The Navy expects to have 15 carriers in its fleet by 1991. To extend the life of its older carriers without building costly new ships, the Navy has launched a program to overhaul major systems in eight of the oldest carriers. The Service Life Extension Program (SLEP) will extend the service life of the carriers from 30 to 45 years.

AIRCRAFT

Aircraft carried aboard carriers, or 'loadings,' vary according to size and mission. Loadings often include two fighter squadrons of F-4s or F-14s or a squadron of F/A-18s and one of A-6s. They also include one anti-submarine-warfare squadron of H-3 Sea King helicopters, RA-5C reconnaissance and EA-6B electronic warfare aircraft, KA-6 tankers, and E-2 airborne early-warning and control aircraft.

The F/A-18 Hornet, the first completely new tactical aircraft in the Navy in more than a dozen years, is three times as reliable as other fighters and features twice the warfare capability. It is also 20 times safer to fly than the aircraft of 30 years ago. It will ultimately replace the F-4 and the A-7 in both the Navy and Marine squadrons.

F-14 Tomcats, the Navy's fastest combat planes, rest on deck awaiting new missions *(opposite)*; two A-7Es from light attack squadron 82 in flight above the USS *Nimitz* (CVN 68) *(above)*; and the nose of an A-6E Intruder peeks from behind a tow tractor working on the USS *John F Kennedy* (CV 67) *(below)*.

It can carry up to 19,000 lb of armament, track multiple targets on its radar and attack eight targets with its air-to-air missiles. Instrumentation in the cockpit has been replaced with essential information displayed at eye level so the pilot can keep his attention on the targets. More than 1300 are planned for the fleet and the Marines.

The F-14 Tomcat is the Navy's most versatile aircraft. These fighters proved themselves in August 1981 when they were attacked by two Libyan aircraft over the Sidra Gulf. The two Tomcats evaded the attackers and downed both with a minimum of effort. The F-14's advanced radar system enables it to track 24 targets at once and attack 6 with Phoenix missiles while scanning the airspace for more targets, which can be destroyed up to 100 miles away.

The F-4 Phantom II is an all-weather defense fighter that flew for the first time in 1958. It has become the backbone of many foreign air forces, including those of Great Britain, Germany, South Korea, Spain, Greece, and Turkey. Production was stopped in 1979 after more than 5000 had been built for the Navy and Air Force. After two decades of service in the fleet, the A-7 Crusader is being replaced with the F/A-18. The A-7 was first flown in 1965.

The A-6E Intruder has been the medium-attack, all-weather mainstay of the Navy and Marine Corps for more than 20 years. It is used for close-in air support and deep-strike missions. Only the aging B-52s of the US Air Force can carry more payload. The A-6E can carry more than 30 types of bombs, rockets, missiles and mines, as well as Harpoon missiles and laser-guided weapons. It is updated constantly with advanced electronics packages.

The EA-6B Prowler is designed for tactical electronic warfare. It is primarily used to jam enemy defense systems during aerial combat. The E-2C Hawkeye is an early-warning aircraft equipped with advanced radar capable of detecting targets within 300 miles and tracking more than 250 aircraft at the same time.

The H-3 Sea King is equipped with sonar, active and passive sonar buoys, magnetic anomaly-detection equipment, and electronic-surveillance-measures equipment to give added protection against missile attack. This helicopter is being phased out in the last half of the 1980s. It has been flown for more than 20 years.

The F-14 (opposite) is the Navy's best fighter-interceptor while the F/A-18 (above) is its best fighter-bomber. A launch officer (below) signals one of them for takeoff from the flight deck of the USS America (CV 66).

A 'Wolfpack' crewman from VF-1 squadron hustles by one of the F-14 Tomcats
aboard the USS *Enterprise* (CVN 65).

Left: The starboard side of the USS *New Jersey* (BB 62) reveals the bridge, forward stack, 5-inch gun turrets and the Vulcan Phalanx close-in weapons system (the white domed object at top center).

Below right: Seamen aboard the same vessel lounge by the aft number three 16-inch turret.

BATTLESHIPS

Reactivation of the *Iowa*-class battleships has permitted the Navy to rapidly expand its fleet without costly new construction. The huge USS *New Jersey* (BB 62) was reactivated into service at less than half the cost of constructing a new frigate. Operating with a carrier battle group and surface-action group, the *New Jersey* is capable of destroying hostile surface targets and shore targets. In amphibious groups, the *New Jersey* can provide protection to other ships in the group, prelanding shore bombardment and additional gunfire support. Although constructed in World War II, the *New Jersey* and her sister ship the USS *Iowa* (BB 61) are not considered old or worn out since both saw limited service and were then 'mothballed' to preserve them. In fact, they are younger than the average ship in the fleet. The USS *New Jersey* has just 13.7 years of service, while the USS *Iowa* has seen only 12.6 years. The historic USS *Missouri* (BB 63), which is scheduled to rejoin the fleet in 1987, has seen just 10.1 years. The USS *Wisconsin* (BB 64), which will return to the fleet in the late 1980s, has just 11.3 years of service.

The four ships in the class are behemoths, displacing 58,000 tons at full load and carrying a crew of about 1900 men. They are almost 888-feet long and 108-feet wide, and are capable of cruising at 33 knots. They have a very long steaming range of 15,000

nautical miles at 17 knots. The most prominent feature of the *Iowa*-class battleships are the three sets of 16-inch main battery guns—two foward and one aft—the largest caliber guns in the world today. (Two Japanese battleships sunk during World War II had 18.1-inch guns.) Each of the nine guns, with well-trained crews, can hurl a 2700-lb piercing projectile on target 20 to 21 miles away every 30 seconds. The projectiles will penetrate 30 feet of reinforced concrete.

The *Iowa*-class battleships are the most heavily armored US warships ever constructed, designed to survive surface-to-surface engagements with enemy ships. The main armor belt consists of 12.1-inch thick steel at its thickest point. Turret faces are 17-inches thick, with tops 7.25-inches thick. Second deck armor is 6-inches thick, while the three-level conning tower sides are 17.3-inches thick.

Interestingly, until the battleships were reactivated, no production facilities were available to manufacture and assemble the 16-inch ammunition

Left: Crew at work below a 16-inch gun turret on an *Iowa*-class battleship.

Below: The armor on the pilot house, 17.3-inches thick, can stop any artillery round or a tactical nuclear weapon.

used by the guns. In addition to new ammunition now in production, there remain thousands of projectiles and charges in storage manufactured during World War II and the Korean War. This stockpile included 12,500 rounds of full-service charges, 12,600 rounds of reduced charges, 15,500 rounds of high-capacity projectiles (which contain less steel and more explosives than the armor-piercing rounds), and 3200 rounds of armor-piercing projectiles. Rounds fired in Vietnam were manufactured in the 1930s and were still in outstanding condition.

The USS *New Jersey* fired 771 main battery rounds during World

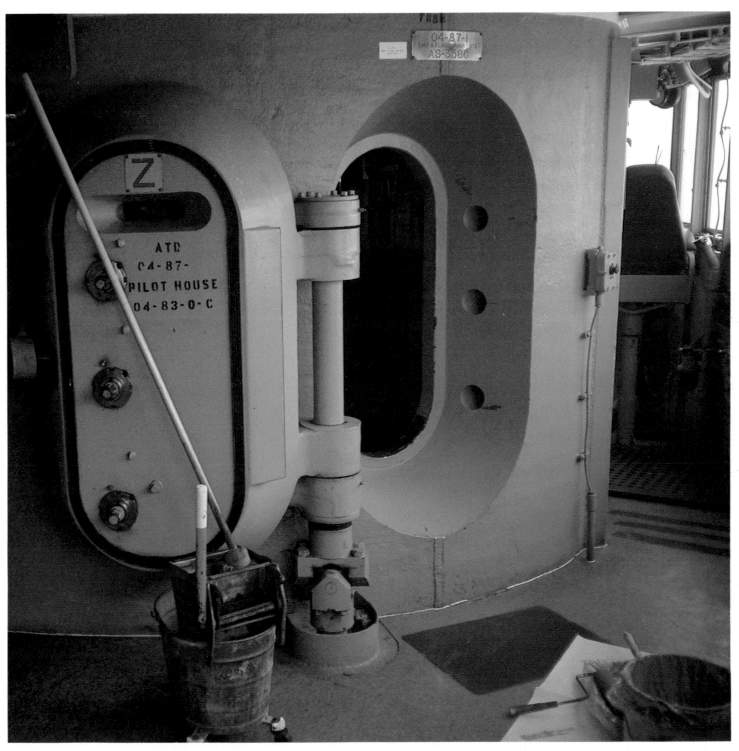

The dawn of a new day backlights the forward main turrets of this battleship beautifully photographed by ship's photographer PH2 Rick Sforza.

War II, 6671 during the Korean War and midshipman courses, and 5688 rounds during the Vietnam conflict. Some 15,000 rounds of 5-inch/38 ammunition were fired from the ship's 10 secondary batteries during its deployment to Vietnam in 1969. An inventory of more than 700,000 rounds of 5-inch/38 ammunition was still available in 1982. The semiautomatic, dual-purpose guns fire at a normal rate of 15-rounds per minute, but the gun's capability for rapid fire can be increased to 22 rounds per minute with a good crew.

The actual range of the 16-inch guns depends on the condition of the large barrels. The USS *New Jersey's* nine barrels averaged 42 percent wear when the ship was reactivated in 1982. The barrels were to have been replaced during the Vietnam War, but wear was greatly reduced with the use of a 'Swedish additive'—a material similar to a Teflon garbage bag was wrapped around the charges to reduce friction in the barrel. In addition to the barrels already installed on the four battleships, 33 barrels remain in storage.

Above: **These seamen well know that painting a ship is a never-ending chore.**

Right: **The USS *New Jersey's* bridge is its nerve center. During WW II it was the flag bridge when the *New Jersey* was Adm Halsey's flagship, but battleships can no longer be designated flagships.**

Each turret is manned by 77 personnel with up to another 36 personnel in each of the turret's six magazines. The large numbers are needed because almost all projectile and powder handling is largely done by hand and machinery.

Despite their awesome firepower, the battleships have been refitted with modern defensive protection, which includes new gunfire-control computers and target-designation systems. Eight Tomahawk armored-box launchers holding 32 cruise missiles have been added to give long-range protection. They have a range of 250 nautical miles when armed with conventional warheads and a modified Harpoon guidance system. The land-attack version with conventional warhead has a 700-mile range and with nuclear warhead a 1500-mile range. The missile

uses an inertial-navigation system with terrain-contour matching for guidance. In addition to the battle-ships, the Navy's cruisers and *Spruance*-class destroyers are getting the same modern defensive system.

For medium-range protection, the battleships are armed with four-can-ister Harpoon launchers carrying 16 surface-to-surface missiles for ship killing. The range of the missile is 70 nautical miles with high-explosive warhead. It searches for the target with its own radar while cruising at about 100 feet above the water. At the end of its flight, it executes a 'pop-up' maneuver to evade close-in enemy defense systems. This also enhances the effectiveness of its warhead. The *Iowas* have also been fitted with four Vulcan Phalanx close-in weapon sys-tems for close-in antimissile defense. This impressive system, consisting of six rotating 20mm barrels controlled electronically, can fire 3000 heavy-metal-penetrating rounds per minute against missiles penetrating air de-fenses.

Navy ships are always prepared for action: The Vulcan Phalanx close-in weapons sytem (CIWS)—known as 'sea whiz'—is potent against aircraft *(left)*; **taking sex-** **tant readings on the port bridge** *(above)*; **the destroyer USS** *Fife* **(DD 991) under way off the starboard side of the battleship USS** *New Jersey* **(BB 62)** *(below)*.

CRUISERS

The Navy has 30 cruisers in its fleet, ranging greatly in age, size and capability. The oldest, the nine cruisers of the *Leahy* class (CG 16), displacing just over 8200 tons at full load, were originally classed as frigates, but have since been rated as guided-missile cruisers (designated CG). All nine were constructed between 1959 and 1964, but were modernized in the late 1960s and early 1970s. They were conceived and built during a period when the Navy had abandoned the gun in favor of the missile. Surface-to-air missile launchers were placed fore and aft, with an 8-tube launcher as the main antisubmarine weapon. These ships have since been

The USS *Leahy* (CG 16) *(above)*, one of the oldest cruisers, is armed with Harpoon and Standard missiles, two Phalanx close-in weapons sytems and two triple torpedo tubes. The USS *Ticonderoga* (CG 47) *(right)*, one of the newest cruisers, is fitted with the Aegis air defense system which can control as many as 18 Standard missiles simultaneously.

refitted with Harpoon and Standard missiles, as well as the Phalanx. They have a ship's complement of 377 men.

Ten conventionally powered ships were originally scheduled in this class, but one was constructed with a nuclear power plant. This is the USS *Bainbridge* (CGN 25), constructed along the same lines as the *Leahy* class, but with a wider hull to handle nuclear reactors. She also is heavier, displacing 8600 tons at full load.

The last conventionally powered warships of their size to be constructed are the *Belknap*-class (CG 26) cruisers, displacing 8200 tons at full load. They have a complement of 418 men. They are antiaircraft and antisubmarine escorts for the carriers, and they were developed from the smaller *Leahys*. When these ships were constructed between 1962 and 1967, the Navy had changed its thinking on putting guns on board. They are

armed with a single 5-inch 54-caliber gun on the aft deck in addition to its missiles and Phalanx. As in the case of the *Leahys*, 10 ships were planned, but Congress insisted a single ship be built with nuclear propulsion. This is the USS *Truxton* (CGN 35), commissioned in 1967. Like her older half-sisters, she is slightly larger to accommodate her two nuclear reactors. She displaces 9127 tons at full load and carries a ship's crew of 498 men. Her

single 5-inch gun is located on the fore deck rather than the aft deck.

The USS *Long Beach* (CGN 9), displacing 17,525 tons, represents two firsts. She was the first of the smaller surface ships to be powered by a nuclear reactor when she was completed in 1961 and the first to depend completely on missiles rather than guns for defense. However, she has since been refitted with two 5-inch guns on her aft superstructure for

defense against low-flying aircraft and low-profile patrol boats. She is also the heaviest cruiser in the fleet, displacing 17,525 tons. She carries a ship's complement of 1160 men.

The two cruisers of the *California* class (CGN 36), both displacing 10,150 tons with a full load, are more fully developed versions of the USS *Bainbridge* (CGN 25) and the USS *Truxton* (CGN 35), but are larger and more advanced. They were funded and built

Left: The nuclear-powered USS *Truxton* (CGN 35) is armed with Harpoon and Standard missiles, antisubmarine rockets, one 5-inch/54-caliber gun and four fixed torpedo tubes.

Below: The USS *Leahy* (CG 16) and other cruisers in its class originally were classed frigates but underwent extensive modernization between 1967-72.

to take advantage of the nuclear-powered carriers. The carriers are worthless without escorts that also can steam for long distances at high speeds without refueling. The two ships carry a crew of 563 men. They are armed with Harpoon and Standard missiles, as well as antisubmarine rockets, two 5-inch guns, six triple torpedo tubes and two Phalanx systems. The Standard missile is a family of missiles designed to be used against ships, aircraft and in-coming missiles. They have a range of about 10 nautical miles.

The four nuclear-powered cruisers of the *Virginia* class (CGN 38) resemble their older half-sisters in the *California* class. They do not have launchers for antisubmarine warfare, which enabled designers to trim 16 feet of hull length from the ships. However, they are armed with multipurpose rocket launchers and triple torpedo tubes fore and aft. Because of Congressional opposition, the *Virginias* will probably be the last nuclear-powered surface ships constructed unless the cost of this technology drops dramatically. However, with its small group of nuclear cruisers in hand, the Navy can deploy a nuclear-powered carrier task force with unlimited cruising range.

The newest cruisers, the three ships of the *Ticonderoga* class (CB 47), are the most advanced in terms of their fighting capabilities. Their sophisticated Aegis surface-to-air defense system gives them an extremely accurate and reliable defense against missiles launched by other ships, submarines, or airplanes. Aegis was designed and developed to integrate electronic detection with the ship's combat missiles. During deployment off the coast of Lebanon in late 1983, the USS *Ticonderoga* detected friendly aircraft in the area, but maintained surveillance, detection and tracking of enemy aircraft. Eleven are to be constructed in this class, which displace 9600 tons with full load. They are powered by four large gas turbines. Each ship has a complement of 360 men.

DESTROYERS

Because US navy ships now carry computers, large and sophisticated radars, large sonars and missile systems, they are larger than ever before. Most classes of Navy ships have doubled in size since World War II.

The *Spruance*-class destroyer USS *Fletcher* (DD 992) dwarfs the two frigates next to it—the USS *McInerney* (FFG 8) and the USS *Marvin Shields* (FF 1066)—yet its ship's complement of 296 men is within 65 men of either of the smaller vessels.

Above: The *Virginia*-class guided missile cruiser USS *Arkansas* (CGN 41) will probably be one of the last nuclear-powered surface ships constructed for the Navy unless the cost of the technology drops to the point where Congress will once more give approval for their building.

Below: The *Charles F Adams*-class guided-missile destroyer USS *Cochrane* (DDG 21), among the oldest destroyers in the fleet, is used primarily for escort duty.

This is especially true of US Navy destroyers. The *Arleigh Burke* (DDG 51) class of destroyers, which will soon go into production, will be the same size as, yet far exceed the fire power of, a World War II cruiser. Despite this increase, it will carry a crew of just 300 men—one-third of those required in the cruiser. Similar manpower savings are evident in the advanced *Spruance-* and *Kidd*-class destroyers and *Oliver Hazard Perry*-class frigates. Manpower reduction has enabled the Navy to operate more efficiently—manpower now represents 30 percent of the 1986 budget compared to 42 percent in 1974. The *Arleigh Burke* class, named after former Chief of Naval Operations Admiral Arleigh Burke of World War II destroyer fame, is designed to replace the *Leahy* and *Belknap* classes of cruisers and the *Farragut* class of guided-missile destroyers. They will be equipped with Aegis, as well as a system to protect their crews against fallout from nuclear, biological and chemical warfare. They are also being constructed with armor and other protection to survive damaging attacks.

The 32 destroyers of the *Spruance* class (DDG 963) were hurriedly constructed to replace a generation of aging World War II-era destroyers that had to be retired in the early 1970s. They are fitted with Harpoon and NATO Sea Sparrow missiles, antisubmarine rockets, two Phalanx systems, two five-inch caliber guns, and two triple torpedo tubes. The first American warships to be powered by gas turbines, they were designed primarily for antisubmarine warfare. They are larger than traditional destroyer designs, displacing 7810 tons. They are also lightly armed, so that they could be constructed rapidly in the large numbers needed by the Navy. The destroyers' lack of weaponry has been widely criticized among Navy personnel, but the modular, rectangular construction of the superstructure will permit new weapons to be installed easily.

The four ships of the *Kidd* class (DDG 993) are closely related to the ships of the *Spruance* class. Displacing 8300 tons and carrying a complement of 338 men, these ships were ordered by the Shah of Iran. The ships were fitted with guided missiles for antiair warfare, a capability not added to the *Spruances*. When the Shah's government fell in 1979, the US Navy took over and completed the ships. However, no more will be added because of their high cost.

The *Charles F Adams* class (DDG 2) of guided-missile destroyers are among the oldest destroyers in the fleet. Constructed between 1958 and 1964, they are updated versions of the now retired *Forrest Sherman*-class designs produced in the postwar period of the 1940s. They displace a modest 4500 tons at full load, and they are used primarily for escort duty. They have a complement of 354 men. There are ten ships in the *Farragut* class (DDG 37), the first ships designed and constructed to carry missiles. They were originally rated as frigates, displace 5300 tons, and carry a crew of 377 men.

It is worth noting that many of the larger surface ships carry helicopters for defensive and tactical purposes. The Navy is now using the SH-2 Seasprite for ASW and antiship and missile operations. The Navy's newest helicopter, the SH-60B Seahawk, better known as the LAMPS (Light Airborne Multipurpose Systems) MkIII helicopter, will soon be deployed aboard most guided-missile destroyers and frigates. The primary mission of this helicopter is to conduct antisubmarine warfare, ship surveillance and targeting, as well as search-and-rescue and medical evacuation. The USS *Underwood* (FFG 36) was the first ship equipped with a production model LAMPS MkIII.

FRIGATES

More than 100 frigates are part of the fleet. Although they provide good protection with their Harpoon and Standard missiles, they remain basically escorts rather than multipurpose warships. The newest frigates, the ships of the *Oliver Hazard Perry* class (FFG 7), represent one of the Navy's best-managed ship-building programs in terms of production and costs. Despite this, the Navy is not seeking more ships in this class because of their limited range and fighting capabilities. Of the 60 planned, only 50 will be constructed. They displace 3585 tons at full load. They are designed to use far fewer men than their older predecessors, the

Opposite: Two views of the USS *Elliott* (DD 967) whose primary mission is anti-submarine warfare (ASW). The basic hull design of *Spruance*-class destroyers provides an unusual potential for growth as improved weapons and electronics systems are developed.

Below: Another *Spruance*-class destroyer, the USS *Fletcher* (DD 992), fires a Harpoon antiship missile.

The *Oliver Hazard Perry*-class guided missile frigate USS *Sides* (FFG 14) is nudged into port by the harbor tug during San Francisco's 1984 Fleet Week Celebration. San Francisco is a long-time Navy town that enthusiastically supports the annual Fleet Week festivities. In the background is the USS *Fletcher* (DD 992).

Knox class (FF 1052), with a ship's complement of 231, including air crew. Although featuring similar layouts with a single hull and shaft, they are powered by two gas turbines that allow them to continue to operate even if one breaks down. They displace 3585 tons.

The *Knox*-class of frigates, the second generation of postwar escort warships, is the largest class of Navy ships constructed since 1945. Forty-six were built in the period between 1965 and 1974, with a single engine and single shaft to make them cheaper. Displacement ranges from 3877 tons full load to 4200 tons full load. Other frigate classes include the *Garcia* (FF 1040), *Bronstein* (FF 1037), *Brooke* (FF 1), and *Glover* (FF 1098) classes. They are of similar size and capabilities.

Above: The USS *Meyerkord* (FF 1058) and the USS *New Jersey* (BB 62).

Below: The missile compartment of the USS *Ohio* (SSBN 726), the first Trident.

Right: The USS *Michigan* (SSBN 727), another Trident-armed 'boomer.'

SUBMARINES

The Navy's fleet of submarines are divided into classes: nuclear-powered ballistic-missile submarines (SSBN) and nuclear attack submarines (SSN). The largest of the SSBNs are the submarines of the *Ohio* class. They displace 18,700 tons, with a length of 560 feet and a beam of 42 feet. Older ships in the SSBN fleet include the older ships of the *Ethan Allen* class, which displace 7880 tons. The submarines of the *Ohio* class carry Trident missiles and four torpedo tubes. They carry a complement of 133 men. Five have been constructed and four more are on order. Even more are expected to be built in the years ahead, despite ongoing opposition from polit-ical opponents within and without the US government. The Trident, a three-staged, solid-fuel rocket, has a range of 4000 nautical miles. It carries thermonuclear Multiple Independently Targetable Re-entry Vehicles (MIRVs) capable of delivering several warheads on individual targets.

Continued on page 74

The launching of the USS *Portsmouth* (SSN 707), one of the *Los Angeles*-class attack submarines yet being produced. Its armament includes Harpoon and Tomahawk missiles, SUBROC, Mk 48 torpedoes and four torpedo tubes. The partially complete USS *Rhode Island* submarine is seen in the background.

Maintenance crew aboard the USS *Enterprise* (CVN 65) ready an F-14 from VF-1, the 'Wolfpack' squadron. In the background is the colorfully marked tail of an F-14 from VF-2, the 'Bounty Hunters' squadron. At the time of this photograph, the two squadrons formed the carrier air wing that deployed to sea together.

The US Navy pioneered nuclear propulsion and submarine warfare in constructing the famed USS *Nautilus* and then experimented with a number of different designs in the hull and nuclear power plants before moving ahead with acceptable designs. *Permit*-class submarines, built in the 1960s, were the first constructed in sizeable numbers and 13 remain in commission. They have been joined by the 20 submarines in the *Sturgeon* class and 37 submarines in the *Los Angeles* class. These two classes are designed to hunt submarines and to protect the SSBNs from underwater attack. They are armed with the Sub-Harpoon and submarine-launched cruise missile systems, as well as conventional and wire-guided torpedoes. Since submarines are tracked by the noise they emit underwater, the two classes are fitted with two contra-rotating propellers on the same shaft to reduce propulsion noise. As a result, these operate more quietly than their Russian counterparts. The Navy is seeking to construct 18 more in the *Los Angeles* class through the end of the

Pegasus-class hydrofoils: USS *Taurus* (PHM 3) (below right); USS *Aguila* (PHM 4) (bottom left); and USS *Pegasus* (PHM 1) on night attack (overleaf). All have speeds of 48 knots when foilborne and a range of over 1200 miles if hullborne—mighty impressive but mighty expensive.

decade. The *Los Angeles*-class subs are 360 feet long and displace 6900 tons. They carry a crew of 127 men. The *Sturgeons* are 292 feet long and displace 4640 tons. They carry a ship's crew of 142.

The two classes are armed with Harpoon and Tomahawk missiles, plus torpedoes. The Mark 48 torpedo, a wire-guided torpedo said to be the most complex torpedo ever developed, is carried by all US Navy submarines. More than 3000 have been delivered. It is about 19 feet long and weighs 3500 lb. It has a range of 23 miles.

OTHER WARSHIPS

One of the more interesting of the smaller warships of the US Navy is one of the most controversial—the *Pegasus* (PHM) class of hydrofoils.

The USS *Cayuga* (LST 1186) whose design is a radical departure from earlier amphibious tank-landing ships. Its 35-ton bow ramp can be lowered onto the beach or married to a causeway to allow rapid unloading of vehicles and equipment. Another ramp extending from the tank deck provides rapid vehicle access to the main deck and bow ramp. Its stern gate provides for the launching and retrieval of amphibious vehicles.

Ships of this class displace just 221 tons at full load and ride above the surface of the water at 48 knots full speed. Six are operating in the Key West area off the coast of Florida. Originally conceived as a NATO ship to be constructed jointly by Germany, Italy and the United States, only six were built. The two European countries withdrew from the project. The ships are armed with eight Harpoon missiles and one 76mm gun. This is an impressive fit of heavy armament on

Opposite and left: **The scissors on the front of the USS** *Cayuga* **(LST 1186) hoist up the landing ramp and a detail of its control house on top of the bridge. (The bumper sticker on the control house reminds us that not all the creatures with whom the** *Cayuga* **shares the sea are made of steel.) In the background** *(opposite)* **is the general-purpose amphibious-assault ship USS** *Peleliu* **(LHA 5) that can carry a complete Marine Battalion Landing Team, their supplies and equipment.**

Below: **Ammunition ship USS** *Haleakala* **(AE 25) displaces 15.5 to 16 tons.**

an extremely fast and maneuverable hull, but the hydrofoils are very expensive to build for their size and range.

The *Iwo Jima, Tarawa* and *Wasp* classes of amphibious-assault ships (LHD, LHA, LPH) represent the Navy's vital and important relationship to the Marine Corps. These ships provide the Marines a viable means of getting from ship to shore by helicopter to augment movement of other troops and equipment by landing craft. The USS *Iwo Jima* (LPH 2) was the first ship designed and constructed to operate helicopters. Each ship can carry a Marine battalion landing team, as well as its weapons and equipment and various support personnel. The USS *Guam* (LPH 9) has operated the Harrier AV-8A V/STOL (Vertical/Short Take-Off and Landing) from its decks. Ships in the *Iwo Jima* class displace 18,000 tons at full load, and the hangar deck can accommodate 20 CH-46 Sea Knight or 11 CH-53 Sea Stallion helicopters.

Austin-class amphibious transport docks such as the USS *Dubuque* (LPD 8) *(right)* and the USS *Denver* (LPD 9) *(below)* can carry 900 troops, up to six CH-46 Sea Knight helicopters and from 4 to 20 landingcraft depending on type.

THE UNITED STATES NAVY IN ACTION

Although the ships of the US Navy have been designed and deployed to counter the threat of the Soviet navy, a major confrontation has never come about. Instead, the Navy has been called upon to safeguard US interests around the globe, especially in troubled hotspots such as the Mediterranean and the waters around the oil-producing countries of the Middle East.

Carriers, though armed with the most powerful weapons of the fleet, often take the backseat to other ships when the Navy is called upon to carry out military assignments. The Navy reactivated the *Iowa*-class battleships so that it could have immense weaponry to deal with an increasingly hostile political and social climate. The Navy realized that these large, powerful warships could serve as showpieces of renewed US determination to maintain its political strength throughout the world.

The decade of the 1980s has been one of flexibility and change for the US Navy as it has been called upon to respond to fast-moving political and hostile conditions around the globe. It has been able to respond with surprising success close to home, as well as in

Opposite: **The battleship USS** ***New Jersey*** **(BB 62) captured on film by ship's photographer PH2 Rick Sforza as it cuts loose with a nine-gun full broadside salvo. Somewhere nine tons of steel will rain down on a target.**

Above: **The breech of one of the** ***New Jersey's*** **big 16-inch guns.**

distant oceans. For example, it was ordered to assist other US Military forces in the waters of the Caribbean in 1983. While steaming toward the Mediterranean to hold exercises, a naval battle group consisting of the USS *Independence*, her escorts and an accompanying Marine Amphibious Ready Group (MARG) were suddenly ordered to assist in the Grenada rescue mission. The Navy played a key role in the invasion of the island and the rescue of American students studying medicine there.

Just eight days later, the same force was directed to the waters off Beirut to conduct reconnaissance flights in the mountains above Beirut at the request of the government of Lebanon. The highlands sheltered guns that were raining fire down on the city. Fighters of the *Independence*, assisted by the large 16-inch guns of the USS *New Jersey*, bombed and shelled suspected terrorist positions. The *New Jersey* was joined by the cruisers USS *Ticonderoga* and USS *Virginia* with their 5-inch guns. The same MARG that had participated in the Grenada operation helped to evacuate 1000 noncombatant Americans and foreign nationals from Lebanese ports using Marine

helicopters and Navy landing craft. The evacuees were then transported by ship to Cyprus.

In the waters of the Red Sea, the surveying ship USS *Harkness* and the amphibious dock-landing ship USS *Shreveport* with her RH-53 mine-clearing helicopters were sent to locate and destroy mines damaging international ships approaching the Suez Canal. Another contingent of RH-53 helicopters, as well as the flagship of the commander of the Middle East, the USS *LaSalle* (AGF 3), were ordered to the area to support the efforts and keep shipping lanes open.

A Navy battle group consisting of destroyers, frigates and submarines has remained stationed in the northern Arabian Sea to monitor on-going hostilities between Iran and Iraq. This force remains on station to protect allied sea lanes and to provide an air warning and defense screen to US-flag tankers under charter to the Military Sealift Command (MSC). The ships steamed to the region after 60 vessels, mostly oil tankers, were hit by aircraft fire between March and December

The USS *New Jersey's* 16-inch guns fire off the coast of Lebanon *(above)*; a sailor has his finger on the trigger of the gun inside turret one *(left)*.

Opposite top: Indian Ocean Task Force under way during the Iran hostage crisis *(from front to back):* carriers USS *Kitty Hawk* (CV 63), USS *Midway* (CV 41) and USS *Nimitz* (CVN 68) with escorts.

Opposite bottom: A crewman aboard the USS *Nimitz* (CVN 68) wears a cold weather face mask during 'Fleetex 82,' a CINCPAC exercise for the US Navy, Air Force, Coast Guard and Canadian Navy.

1984. The tactics were not like those conducted during convoys across the Atlantic. The warships established a radar screen from the Strait of Hormuz in Bahrain to the Persian Gulf. This task group has enabled the Navy to protect its oil shipments to the island of Diego Garcia in the Indian Ocean and the US naval base at Subic Bay in the Philippines.

The shipping lanes through the Indian Ocean are among the world's most critical. Because of this, the Navy now maintains a continual presence in the region. During 1984, the air

craft carrier USS *Ranger* and her battle group operated in this region and set a record for continuous operations for a conventionally powered carrier battle group. They remained at sea for 121 days and steamed more than 50,000 miles. During the course of this deployment, the Navy concluded the first visit to an Indian port by a US naval warship in 13 years.

It was recognized in the late 1970s that the Military Sealift Command could not adequately respond to emergencies, especially in distant places like the Indian Ocean. Recognizing the

lack of sealift capability, the Carter administration ordered the Navy to preposition a small force of ships and supplies at Diego Garcia. Owned by Great Britain, the island had already been used as a base for some years on a small scale by the US. The prepositioned force consists of 17 ships, including a water tanker, ammunition ship and cargo ships of various types. They have been given the designation of the Near-Term Preposition Force (NTPF), and are loaded with petroleum, oil and lubricants, as well as water. Four are designed to carry vehicles and one carries a hospital designed for 500 men. They can sustain a Marine force of 12,500 men for 30 days. One third of the force is under way at all times, and all ships get under way every three months and participate in convoy exercises. Fifteen of the ships are chartered, while two are owned by the government. They are maintained in such a state of readiness that they can get under way in two hours when in port.

The Navy also maintains visibility in the waters off the coast of Central

America, where it monitors arms shipments from the Soviet Bloc to countries such as Cuba and Nicaragua. The fleet has conducted numerous exercises there to demonstrate US resolve to support neighbors and allies against Communist insurgency movements.

US Navy ships have also been used to help obstruct the flow of illegal drugs into the United States. Navy support of a major US Coast Guard drug-interdiction operation in the Caribbean Sea in 1983 resulted in the seizure of 24 vessels carrying illegal drugs.

On the moonless night of 10 October 1985, high over the eastern Mediterranean Sea, six US Navy F-14 Tomcats launched from the USS *Saratoga* intercepted, then forced down, an

The ever-vigilant Navy: A carrier crewman *(top)* signals to the guided-missile frigate cruising alongside; pilots of the SH-60 Sea Hawks *(above)* patrol for hostile submarines; and F-14s set out on a sunset mission *(opposite).*

Egyptian Boeing 737 at a NATO base near Sigonella on the island of Sicily. They had been ordered aloft by the direct orders of President Ronald Reagan. The 737 carried four members of the Palestinian Liberation Organization who had hijacked an Italian cruise ship, the *Achille Lauro*. For two days, they had held 500 passengers hostage including dozens of Americans. They murdered a 69-year-old handicapped US citizen and threw his body overboard along with his wheelchair.

The orders to intercept came while the USS *Saratoga* was steaming northwest in the waters of the Adriatic Sea near the coast of Albania. She turned south and prepared to launch the six planes, which were sent aloft with two E-2C radar planes and two air tankers for refueling.

Just after midnight, the Tomcats spotted the 737 near the island of Crete after it had lifted off from Egypt. It was a difficult mission to spot the 737 in the crowded skies above the Mediterranean, but US officials credited a steady flow of accurate intelligence for the Navy's ability to single out the plane from the other commercial jets.

The Navy F-14s had been launched even before the 737 had left a military base outside Cairo and were waiting over Crete. They shadowed the plane while it was denied permission to land in Tunis, Tunisia and Athens, Greece. Then they surrounded the aircraft on four sides and signaled it to land in Sicily, with the permission of the Italian government.

The pilot of the 737, who was in radio contact with the US Navy fighters, agreed to land in Sicily. No shots were fired. When the plane touched down, it was greeted by specially trained US troops who were at the base. The four terrorists were arrested by Italian officials, along with the Egyptian crew of the plane.

It was an unusual assignment for

The USS *Kitty Hawk* (CV 63) enters San Francisco Bay with Coast Guard escort for Fleet Week 83 *(below)*. A crewman mans the helm of the *Kitty Hawk (opposite top)* which displaces 80,800 tons fully loaded and carries about 95 aircraft.

The rallying call of the Navy bugleman has sounded for over two centuries. Today's Navy remains committed to the Navy's founding purpose—guarding the maritime interests of the United States by keeping the sea lanes open.

the Navy and its aviators, but it was one carried out quietly and successfully. It was a mission that showed the daring and flexibility of the US Navy.

THE UNITED STATES NAVY TODAY

Today's US Navy is an ever-changing naval force on the world's oceans. When it was created more than 200 years ago, it was designed to protect US maritime interests not only close to home but on the high seas far from home. That mission remains as true today as it did during the period of the Revolutionary War. It is a naval force in transition, with several new ships of advanced design and weaponry joining the fleet and veteran ships departing for the scrap yard as they come to the end of their service lives.

The Navy today is under challenge and test, especially from its shadowy and threatening opponent, the Soviet navy. In recent years, ships of the Soviet fleet have been deployed nearly everywhere on the globe, including the waters of the Western Hemisphere where the threat has moved very close to home for the US. Off the coast of Central America, the Soviet Union has sent numerous task-force fleets consisting of guided missile helicopter cruisers and destroyers.

As the Soviets have increased the size of their navy, they have been more willing to embark on military adventures far from their homeland. It is now a navy designed for offensive action—to cut off the free flow of trade and commerce in the event of war. The US remains a naval power by necessity, dependent upon imports of goods and strategic materials vital to its economy. The seas are the lifeblood of the United States. It is for this reason that the modern Navy has been designed to keep these sea lanes open.

The Navy remains an ever-vigilant force. It must be prepared to venture into harm's way when necessary and control the seas to assure access for the United States and its allies. In the words of US Secretary of Defense Caspar Weinberger: 'We know that strength alone is not enough, but without it there can be no effective diplomacy and peace. Conversely, weakness and hopeful passivity are only self-defeating. They invite the very aggression and instability they would seek to avoid.'

INDEX

Below: The *Virginia*-class guided missile cruiser USS *Arkansas* (CGN 41) in San Francisco Bay.

Overleaf: The Navy's high-energy laser beam director, an experimental system that tracks targets in flight and directs a beam to selected aimpoints. When it is mated with the Navy's high-energy chemical laser it promises to be a most potent tool.

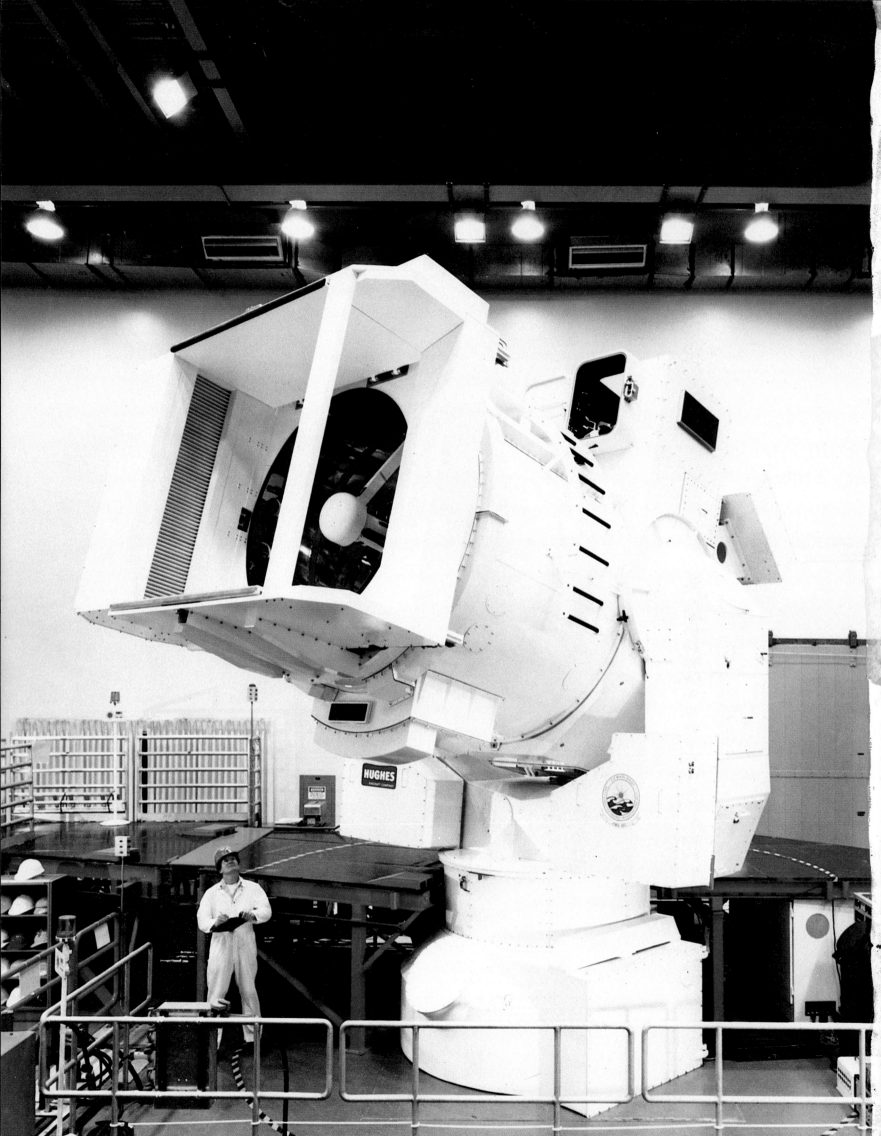